Stop Struggling and Start Thriving: A Guide To Transform Your Law Firm

Design and cover art by Kelley Brubaker.

ISBN: 979-8851445279

Successful implementation and adherence to the Profit First methodology are solely dependent on the business implementing Profit First.

The ideas and content within this course are being shared with the express permission of Mike Michalowicz and Profit First Professionals.

Table of Contents

Introduction 1

The Problem In Your Business: A Broken Formula . 9

    A Lesson In Human Behavior 12

    Back To "Bank Balance Accounting" 14

    OK...How Does This Help You?......................16

    Make It Happen 18

Phase I - The Profit Assessment........................19

    Part A - Historical Review................................19

    Part B - Where You Want To Be 25

    Part C - Roll Out Plan......................................31

Phase II - The Implementation 34

    Allocations 40

    The Last Two New Accounts (For Now).........42

Phase III – Profit Points For Profit Maximization .. 44

    Expense Analysis 45

    Pricing..52

    Margin..59

    Efficiency 68

    Leveraging Potential Client Interest................74

    Prospects 81

    New Clients..87

    Matters...93

Marketing ROI 98

Accounts Receivable 101

Which Profit Point did you find to be the most
profound to your business?.................................103

About The Author...105

Free Resources..109

Introduction

Are you an attorney struggling to make a profit? Frustrated that your bank balance does not reflect more zeros from all the demanding work you do for your clients? Do you miss having a life outside of the office? Is it difficult enjoying time with your kids because you are worrying about your firm and clients all the time?

If so, you are not alone. In fact, many law firms struggle to turn an adequate profit, despite bringing in significant revenue. The anxiety it creates bleeds into every aspect of your life.

I am here to tell you that it does not have to be this way for you! And, yes, I am being serious. Sadly, there is not a magical potion available. And, it will take some work. But this is fruitful work with tangible proof: more money in the bank.

The reason for your current situation is simple: gross revenue does not matter if you are not profitable at the end of the day. To truly be successful, you need to focus on growing your bottom line, not your top line.

I do not have a quick or easy solution for you. Like anything in life, the best things do not come for free. But, fortunately for you, there is a way to put your firm on the right path to help you achieve your business (and personal) goals.

I am going to be upfront with you. This book exists for two reasons:

- Reason #1: So that you will eventually hire me and my team to help you implement everything you read here and more.

- Reason #2: To get you results **in advance** so that you will want to do Reason #1 as quickly as possible.

Throughout this book, you will find me being candid and honest with you. I want to help anyone who reads this book achieve the ultimate goal of eradicating entrepreneurial poverty. Payoff all my debt and a grow my bank balance without working myself to death? Sign me up!

I want you to realize that to achieve something new, something new must take place. Remember the definition of insanity? Insanity is doing the same thing repeatedly, expecting *different* results.

This is going to be a different process than you are used to. That is why it works. That is why it is going to give you different results than you have ever experienced.

I have structured this book as follows:

First, I want you to get an honest picture of where your business is financially today. Based on the struggles I have experienced in my business and witnessed in my client's businesses over the years, I am willing to bet money that your current struggles are simply a symptom of habits you have adopted over the years that you did not realize were sabotaging your business.

After that, I will teach you how your firm could be financially different. Along with a path to get you from today to your goals.

Finally, we will spend a lot of time focusing on various aspects of your business that you may be neglecting or simply did not know you should be periodically monitoring. We will work to get your firm on the correct path to achieve its maximum profit potential.

It might sound like a lot, but really, the entirety of this book can be summed up in the following three points.

Point #1

You need to know where your business has been before you can determine your path to the financial future you desire. Without a clear understanding of your financial past, it would be impossible to set your business on the path to the prosperous future it deserves.

You will get clarity on where you've been.

Point #2

There is no doubt about it, humans are a complicated species. We like to think that we are rational beings, but the truth is that we're often driven by instinct.

Understanding basic human instincts and how you can use them to your advantage will make it easier for you to transform your business into your dream firm.

You will see what is possible to achieve financially with your firm.

Point #3

It has been said that the journey of a thousand miles begins with a single step. The same can be said of financial success.

Too often, people get discouraged because they do not see immediate results from their efforts. However, small changes can create an avalanche of positive energy that will be reflected in a growing bank balance. A growing bank balance that will feed your firm to reach your goals.

You will get practical and straightforward ideas for how you can achieve your firm's financial goals.

The information you are about to discover has radically transformed my life for the better, with benefits far beyond the financial. I hope you will be able to make the connection for yourself as well.

It is a great privilege to share what I know with you. I hope it inspires and informs you to grow and improve your own business, so you can grow and improve the lives of others.

If you read this book and decide you'd like help implementing its strategies as quickly as possible, please book a call to chat with me by going here:

ProfitScaleThrive.com/contact

To a brighter future,

Kelley

The Problem In Your Business: A Broken Formula

The Broken Formula is Sales – Expenses = Profit.

A study by the Small Business Association (SBA), concluded that of 28 million small businesses in the US, a staggering 22 million of them (approximately 80%) are break-even and surviving check to check.

And, guess what? They all use this formula. We were given the incorrect method to manage our business. It is called "Generally Accepted Accounting Principles" or GAAP for short. The profit formula it states is Sales - Expenses = Profit.

It is a lie.

For years we have been doing it all wrong because accounting alone focuses on the numbers, yet it ignores the human behavior around the numbers. But do not worry because:

1. It is not your fault.

2. You are not alone.

3. It is easily fixable.

Let me ask you a question. When was the last time you looked at your P&L? What about this question: How often do you look at your bank balance?

Many entrepreneurs manage cash flow via "bank balance accounting" (looking at their online bank balance) instead of looking at their P&L.

Before we learn more about bank balance accounting, let us talk about human behavior for a moment.

A Lesson In Human Behavior

Parkinson's Law is a clever way to illustrate how work expands to fill the time allotted for its completion. First coined in 1955 by Cyril Northcote Parkinson, this humorous essay on his experiences at The Economist revealed just what can happen when you are stuck with too many projects and not enough hours- he named it after himself!

Simply put, Parkinson's Law states 'Our demand upon a resource tends to expand to match the supply of that resource.'

Applied to your business:

- in terms of time, when you have a brief due in 3 weeks, it will take you 3 weeks to get it filed but the same brief due tomorrow will get filed tomorrow.

- in terms of money, when you have a lot of money in the bank, you will spend it. If you do not have much money in the bank, you will be frugal with your spending.

Think about Parkinson's Law in your daily life. It dictates our use of toothpaste, paper towels, and even toilet paper as well as time and money! It surrounds us everywhere.

Back To "Bank Balance Accounting"

While we know we *should* read our P&L, Cash Flow, and Balance Sheet regularly, conduct a financial analysis, and reconcile our General Ledger accounts, the reality is that we do not.

We check our bank balance online. Constantly.

Tying this to Parkinson's Law: as our deposits increase so does our spending and vice versa.

Parkinson's Law becomes a powerful ally when you take your profit first and are forced to grow your business off the remainder.

This is why the Sales - Expenses = Profit formula is wrong.

In the past, profit was what was left over. Now expenses are forced to adjust to what remains after profit.

Now 'bank balance accounting' has become a highly effective method of managing your finances.

"Profit First" rewrites the GAAP formula to:

Sales - Profit = Expenses

OK...How Does This Help You?

What is Profit First? Profit First is a book written by Mike Michalowicz about how to manage the cashflow of a business. Many business owners I speak with believe Profit First to be an accounting system that focuses on reducing expenses. It is not.

It is a cash management system. It is a way to work on increasing revenue while managing expenses to increase your net profit, which ultimately means a growing bank balance. Actual cash in the bank.

In other words, Profit First is a simple but effective system that will help any law firm become more profitable.

Once you have Profit First in place, you'll be able to see exactly where your money is going and make informed decisions about where to allocate your resources. This will help you grow your bottom line and achieve financial success.

The easiest part is that once set up, you can check the financial health of your business by glancing at your bank balances online...which you already do.

You can buy and read the entire Profit First book from Amazon, but I am going to summarize it for you in the following chapters as well as give you tips and tricks not in the book!

Make It Happen

Profit First is implemented in three phases.

1. **Phase I – The Profit Assessment** – A historical review of your company's financial trends, matched to the best financially performing companies, with a plan, "Roll Out Plan", on how to get your business there.

2. **Phase II - The Implementation** – The setup of allocation bank accounts and immediate allocation percentages of profit and other funds.

3. **Phase III – Profit Maximization** – An ongoing process of continual profit, owner's pay, and other improvements. Leverage Parkinson's Law to build maximum efficiencies and innovations in your business.

Phase I - The Profit Assessment

Part A - Historical Review

1. Identify your company's Real Revenue* for the last 12 months.

2. Pick the column that corresponds to your Real Revenue in Figure 1.

3. Complete the Actual column in Figure 2 with your actual numbers for the last 12 months.

4. Using the percentages identified in Step 2, fill out the PF% in Figure 2.

5. Multiply the Real Revenue number in the Actual column with each PF% and enter the resultant number in the corresponding PF$ row.

6. For each row, subtract the PF$ number from the Actual number and put the result in the corresponding row in the Bleed column. Note: You may get negative numbers.

7. For the Fix column put the word "Increase" if the corresponding row contains a negative number and the word "Decrease" if it is a positive number.

RESULT: The completed Instant Assessment tells you what you need to do with your allocation of money (either Increase or Decrease) and by how much (specified in The Bleed column) for each account.

*Real Revenue – Real Revenue is the income generated by your company after subtracting the cost of materials and subcontractors. This is like Gross Profit but does not include your employee labor. The total income of a service business is typically its Real Revenue. The total income for a retailer, manufacturer, or agency (with many subcontractors) typically needs to adjust the total income to Real Revenue.

FIGURE 1 – Target Allocation Percentages (TAPs)

Real Revenue Range	A $0– $250K	B $250K – $500K	C $500K – $1M	D $1M – $5M	E $5M – $10M	F $10M – $50M
Real Revenue	100%	100%	100%	100%	100%	100%
Profit	5%	10%	15%	10%	15%	20%
Owner's Pay	50%	35%	20%	10%	5%	0%
Tax	15%	15%	15%	15%	15%	15%
Operating Expenses	30%	40%	50%	65%	65%	65%

FIGURE 2 – Current Allocation Percentages (CAPs)

	ACTUAL	PF%	PF$	THE BLEED	THE FIX
Top Line Revenue					
Material & Subs					
Real Revenue		100%			
Profit					
Owner's Pay					
Tax					
Operating Expenses					

I do these calculations frequently when working with clients. For my own efficiency, I simplified this step with a spreadsheet that I am happy to share with you. **Page 109 shares instructions on how you can obtain a copy of my spreadsheet for yourself.**

Part B - Where You Want To Be

We now know where you have been. And, if you were happy with those results, you would not be reading this book. So, here are the million-dollar questions you need to answer:

- What do you **need** from your business?

- What do you **want** from your business?

To determine your **need**, we can calculate your minimum acceptable owner's compensation with the form in Figure 3 below.

FIGURE 3 – What You Need (Minimum Compensation)

1. Answer the questions below labeled A thru D by placing your answer in the blue boxes.

A. Use this drop down to select your GROSS annual revenue this year > [0 - 250k]

B. How many billable HOURS do you want to work each WEEK? [30] hours/week

C. How many WEEKS do you want to work ANNUALLY? [40] weeks/year

D. How much do you need for personal expenses? Enter amounts in the column that corresponds to the frequency you make cash payment.

Personal Expenses	Monthly	Quarterly	Semi-Annually	Annually
Car - Gas/Fuel	$ 290			
Car Insurance				$ 900
Car Loan	$ 550			
Car Maintenance		$ 75		
Cell Phone	$ 90			
Childcare and/or School Activities				$ 250
Clothing		$ 100		
Dining Out	$ 500			
Education Savings for Children	$ 200			
Groceries	$ 500			
Health Insurance	$ 500			
Home Entertainment (Cable, Satellite, Netflix, Diarco, Hulu)	$ 85			
Home Improvement Projects		$ 500		
Home Insurance, if not included in mortgage payment				$ 100
Internet	$ 55			
Investments (Stocks, Bonds, CDs, Property)	$ 500			
Medical Out Of Pocket (co pays, prescriptions)	$ 60			
Mortgage/Rent	$ 2,400			
Real Estate Taxes, if not included in mortgage payment				$ 18,000
Retirement Savings				
Student Loan				
Tuition Payments for Children				
Utilities (gas, water, electric, sewer, propane, trash)	$ 500			
Vacation				$ 6,000
Other				
Other				
Other				
Total Cash Needed Annually				**103,630**

2. To PROFITABLY reach your goal of working...

30 billable hours per week
40 weeks per year

Your hourly billable rate needs to be a MINIMUM of: $ 173

3. What could Profit-First look like in your business?

Minimum Gross Annual Revenue Needed To Fund Personal Expenses $ 207,260

	Profit	Owner's Pay	Tax	OpEx
Profit-First Allocation %	5%	50%	15%	30%
Amounts You'd Have in One Year	$ 10,363	$ 103,630	$ 31,089	$ 62,178

4. "How we spend our days is, of course, how we spend our lives." Annie Dillard

So here is what your time is worth...

For a total annual gross revenue of: $ 207,260
Value of your time per work week: $ 5,182
Value of your time per work hour: $ 173
Value of your time per one work minute: $ 2

Are you spending your time wisely?

6 minute phone call: $ 17
12 minute interruption: $ 35
18 minutes on email: $ 52
24 minutes on social media: $ 69
30 minutes drafting a blog post: $ 86
60 minute networking meeting: $ 173

Page 109 shares instructions on how you can obtain a copy of my spreadsheet for yourself.

To determine your **want**, I can offer guidance but only you can decide for sure.

Example wants:

- Reducing work hours in half while doubling my income
- Going on vacation annually without going in debt to pay for it
- Being able to volunteer time to my kid's … (e.g., PTA, little league coach, etc.)
- Take one day off per week to learn a new skill or hobby (e.g., horseback riding, ballroom dancing, drawing, etc.)

Now, compare your historical data (Figure 2) to the financial need of your business (Figure 3). How does this compare to what you want from your business?

I will be honest, my first go-round on this step was ugly. I honestly felt like I would never make Profit First work for me.

Changing my money mindset to take my profit first and taking things day by day, week by week, and quarter by quarter has led me to the financially strong business that I have today.

In my personal life, I am a single mom with minimal financial support from my ex-husband. I do have a mortgage payment for a house we bought together when I was purposely working part time and our agreement was I would contribute 50% for it and now (unplanned) I pay 100% for it, but I have no credit card debt.

I was able to put half down in cash without a trade-in on a $45,000 vehicle I purchased in 2021 which will reduce my total cost (with lower interest paid over the life of the loan). My goal was to pay 100% cash for a new car, but my old car had high mileage and during the pandemic when there was a car shortage, I panicked that I would be immobile for weeks if my car died (I live in the countryside without public transit).

And this year for spring break, I took my girls to Disneyland - paid for in advance with cash from my profit distributions (not on credit cards).

This really does work.

Part C - Roll Out Plan

Rome was not built in a day, and your profit account will not be, either. A slow and steady implementation of Profit First will help you reach your Target Allocation Percentages (TAPs) without backsliding into old behaviors. Your custom Roll Out Plan will be your roadmap on this journey.

FIGURE 4 – Roll Out Plan

Rollout Plan

Prepared for: ____________
Prepared by: ____________
Date prepared: ____________

Presented by Profit Scale Thrive
www.ProfitScaleThrive.com

Cells highlighted in **BLUE** require manual input.

CAPs current quarter %s -------> progress with baby steps ---------> reach target %s from Profit First book

	+/-	3Q22	4Q22	1Q23	2Q23	3Q23	4Q23	1Q24	2Q24
Profit CAP	1%	2%	3%	4%	5%	6%	7%	8%	9%
Owner's Comp CAP	2%	26%	28%	30%	32%	34%	36%	38%	40%
Tax CAP	1%	2%	3%	4%	5%	6%	7%	8%	9%
Operating Expense CAP	--%	70%	66%	62%	58%	54%	50%	46%	42%
Extra Account #1 CAP	0%	0%	0%	0%	0%	0%	0%	0%	0%
Extra Account #2 CAP	0%	0%	0%	0%	0%	0%	0%	0%	0%
Extra Account #3 CAP	0%	0%	0%	0%	0%	0%	0%	0%	0%
Extra Account #4 CAP	0%	0%	0%	0%	0%	0%	0%	0%	0%

Notes:
Use this calculator after preparing your Profit Assessment. This calculator is your guide to get you from your current state to running optimally in accordance with Profit First.

Extra accounts are to support Chapter 9 - Profit First: Advanced Techniques.

Each quarter, on the 10th/25th (or your chosen allocation dates), enter the date, balance of your income account (=Real Revenue), and the allocation amounts will calculate for you.

															Quarterly Totals
Allocation Date		8/4/2022													
Current balance of your Income Account		$ 2,581													
Minimum balance required in your bank account	$ 10	$ (10)	$ -	$ -	$ -	$ -	$ -	$ -	$ -	$ -	$ -	$ -	$ -	$ -	
Amount to Allocate out of income account		$ 2,571	$ -	$ -	$ -	$ -	$ -	$ -	$ -	$ -	$ -	$ -	$ -	$ -	$ 2,571
This quarter's CAPs from your Rollout Plan above	3Q22														
To Profit	2%	$ 51.42	$ - .00	$ - .00	$ - .00	$ - .00	$ - .00	$ - .00	$ - .00	$ - .00	$ - .00	$ - .00	$ - .00	$ - .00	$ 51
To Owner's Comp	26%	$ 668.46	$ - .00	$ - .00	$ - .00	$ - .00	$ - .00	$ - .00	$ - .00	$ - .00	$ - .00	$ - .00	$ - .00	$ - .00	$ 668
To Tax	2%	$ 51.42	$ - .00	$ - .00	$ - .00	$ - .00	$ - .00	$ - .00	$ - .00	$ - .00	$ - .00	$ - .00	$ - .00	$ - .00	$ 51
To OPEX	70%	$ 1,799.70	$ - .00	$ - .00	$ - .00	$ - .00	$ - .00	$ - .00	$ - .00	$ - .00	$ - .00	$ - .00	$ - .00	$ - .00	$ 1,800
To Extra #1	0%	$ - .00	$ - .00	$ - .00	$ - .00	$ - .00	$ - .00	$ - .00	$ - .00	$ - .00	$ - .00	$ - .00	$ - .00	$ - .00	$ -
To Extra #2	0%	$ - .00	$ - .00	$ - .00	$ - .00	$ - .00	$ - .00	$ - .00	$ - .00	$ - .00	$ - .00	$ - .00	$ - .00	$ - .00	$ -
To Extra #3	0%	$ - .00	$ - .00	$ - .00	$ - .00	$ - .00	$ - .00	$ - .00	$ - .00	$ - .00	$ - .00	$ - .00	$ - .00	$ - .00	$ -
To Extra #4	0%	$ - .00	$ - .00	$ - .00	$ - .00	$ - .00	$ - .00	$ - .00	$ - .00	$ - .00	$ - .00	$ - .00	$ - .00	$ - .00	$ -
Edit Checks ->	Allocation - 100%	Allocation - 100%	Allocation - 100%	Allocation - 100%	Allocation - 100%	Allocation - 100%	Allocation - 100%	Allocation - 100%	Allocation - 100%	Allocation - 100%	Allocation - 100%	Allocation - 100%	Allocation - 100%	Allocation - 100%	

Page 109 shares instructions on how you can obtain a copy of my spreadsheet for yourself.

Phase II - The Implementation

Remember when I mentioned human behavior at the beginning of this book? This is where that conversation will become relevant. Profit First is based on the old school "envelope method" or newly termed "cash stuffing method" of cash management.

This means that for every dollar that comes into your firm, we have pre-determined how that money is going to work for you based on your CAPs from Figure 4.

So, how is this going to work?

The next step is going to sound painful, but I promise, it is not. You need to get your 5 foundational bank accounts opened. Whereas the traditional, old school envelope method used literal envelopes, Profit First uses bank accounts to segregate the money based on the purpose you have assigned it.

This treatment is exactly how your IOLTA account functions in your firm today. The IOLTA account exists to keep your trust fund money separate from your firm's operating funds. Each bank account will work the same way: keep your profit separate from your owner's compensation separate from your tax money separate from your operating expenses.

If your bank charges monthly fees or requires a substantial minimum balance per account to waive monthly fees, please refer to this listing of Profit First friendly financial institutions to find a provider with low or, ideally, no fees.

Page 109 shares instructions on how you can obtain a copy of my listing of Profit First Friendly Banks.

When I opened my accounts, I sent an email to my local branch manager letting her know I needed 4 new business checking accounts opened (since I already had one in use).

Because I was an existing bank customer, she already had my business and personal info needed to open these accounts. She called me when she had the paperwork ready, and it took me less than 15 minutes to sign the necessary papers to open the new accounts.

Word of advice - use your existing bank account as your income account because it is easier to change your existing auto-payments from this account than it is to redirect your deposits from clients who pay you by ACH, EFT, wire, or credit card.

If you find it unimaginable to do this step, I offer two alternatives:

1. If you use QuickBooks Online, open a "QuickBooks Checking Account" directly through QBO. This account features "envelopes" to put your money into buckets. Currently, you can create up to 9 envelopes. You can use these envelopes as your 5 foundational Profit First accounts.

2. Find a non-traditional, internet-based bank that understands Profit First. At

the time of this publication, Relay Financial is the official bank partner of Profit First. They understand and support Profit First. They make it easy (and I mean EASY) to set up the bank accounts you need to manage Profit First.

If you want to try Relay - **page 109 shares instructions on how you can obtain links referenced in the book**. While it is an affiliate link - I promise that it costs you nothing and I may receive a financial incentive if you open an account at Relay, but my true incentive to share this link with you is that you will have a dedicated account manager to help get you onboarded with Relay.

Once your 5 accounts are established, make your first allocations using your Current Allocation Percentages (CAPs) from Figure 4.

Allocations

The last step of this phase is to determine how often you will be making your allocations. The book suggests making your allocations on the 10th and 25th of each month and Mike explains why in the book. Personally, this does not work well for me.

The best practice is to make allocations weekly or bi-weekly. I suggest making the allocations as part of your payroll process assuming you run payroll every week or every other week.

While I initially used a local bank, when the partnership with Relay Fi was announced, I moved all my business accounts to Relay Fi. The advantage is that Relay Fi lets me set up an automatic transfer rule based on my CAPs (percentage based, not a fixed dollar amount), and I set up the transfers to happen every Monday.

If you do not run payroll, I would suggest linking the allocation process to your frequency of paying your bills. Consistency is key with your allocations, so they become a habit. Make at least two allocations per month or up to four. I have had clients make allocations every few days, but I do not think the cost-benefit is worth that high of a frequency.

The Last Two New Accounts (For Now)

We are not done opening bank accounts though. You will need two business accounts at a **hard for you to access** bank. These accounts are critical. It will prevent you from "robbing Peter to pay Paul."

These accounts can be either a checking or savings account. One will become your long-term profit account and the other will be your long-term tax account.

After your initial allocations are completed, transfer the entire balance of your profit account to the long-term profit account. Repeat for your tax balance.

This step is critical because of our nature for bank balance accounting! You will routinely check the balance of your accounts at your **main** bank. These two additional accounts, you will soon forget you have.

Out of sight = out of mind until every quarter-end when it is time for your profit distribution, or your estimated tax payment is due.

Phase III – Profit Points For Profit Maximization

For me, here is where the fun part begins. A common misconception about Profit First is that the methodology focuses entirely on reducing expenses.

While expense reduction is *one* focus of Profit First, there are a few additional opportunities to improve the profitability of your business. We call these "Profit Points".

Magical synergy happens when you take time to work through the following Profit Points.

Expense Analysis

- When was your last comprehensive and in-depth analysis of the expenses on your P&L?

If you are like most people, you probably don't give much thought to how you spend your money. You just swipe your card and go about your business.

But what if you stopped to take a closer look at your expenses? Would you be surprised to find that you are spending money on things that you don't really need?

It is time to start taking a magnifying glass to every penny you spend and evaluating whether those expenses are necessary.

Start with dues, memberships, subscriptions, continuing education, training, and professional development. Are you really using all the benefits that these memberships offer? Or could you get by without them? Do you really need to attend that out-of-town conference? Or can you get the same information from a webinar or online course?

If you are not careful, these seemingly small expenses can add up quickly.

In all, you will need to review all your expenditures for at least the last 12 months, but ideally for the last 24. Look for recurring transactions. Pay attention to the frequency. Be honest with yourself - are you fully using each membership or subscription? Is there an opportunity to downgrade a membership or subscription so you still have access to it, but at a lower cost?

When I did this exercise for my business, I also did it for my personal expenditures too. So, the best example I think most can relate to is my Sirius XM subscription. I have had a Sirius subscription since 2006. I automatically selected the top plan because of FOMO. I could not imagine having the subscription and not having access to every station.

At least I did pay for the annual subscription to save about 10% over the monthly pricing. The subscription is automatically renewed every year. It was on autopilot. When I did this exercise, I realized that for the top tier plan, I only listened to ONE of the extra stations in that tier. One. It was one I could easily do without too. It was easy to jump online to downgrade my account.

I was able to keep my Sirius XM subscription at a lower price. Win. Ultimately, I realized upon a subsequent expense review that I was listening to Spotify more than Sirius XM and with my new vehicle, I could plug my phone into the sound system. I was able to eliminate Sirius XM completely for additional savings. Winning!

How much can you save by doing the same thing?

- Do you have a system in place to track your expenses and verify the return on them?

Per investopedia.com, Return on Investment (ROI) is calculated by subtracting the initial value of the investment from the final value of the investment (which equals the net return), then dividing this new number (the net return) by the cost of the investment, then finally, multiplying it by 100.

Most likely, many of your expenses will not have a calculable ROI. I suggest gauging your gut reaction when you review your expenses periodically. If an expense is something you just cannot live without AND you benefit from it on a routine basis, keep it. If you can live without it, cut it.

A lot of people think that frugality means cheap and that living within your means is all about depriving yourself of the things you want. But that is not true! If there is something you really want or need and it brings you joy on a regular basis, then, keep it in your budget! On the other hand, if there is something you can live without, do not be afraid to cut it out. Just because you have always had a certain expense does not mean you have to keep it forever. Be mindful of your spending and make decisions that will help you save money in the long run. After all, financial peace of mind is priceless.

- By what percentage do you think you could cut your expenses without causing harm to your business?

With every client I work with, I start the challenge at 10%. Can you cut 10% of your total expenses? How much would that be for you in dollars? I have seen many start-up firms running so lean that it was impossible to cut 5%, but I've seen many firms bleeding so much that 25% was easy to identify and cut.

While I am challenging you to find and eliminate 10% of your expenses, do your honest best. It is to your benefit.

Pricing

- When was your last fee increase?

If it has been a while, it might be time for a small hike. Adjusting for inflation, the cost of living has gone up since you last raised your fees. In addition, your services are worth more now than they were a few years ago. You have gained experience and skills over time.

By raising your fees, you can ensure that you are being fairly compensated for the value you provide.

If it has been more than 12 months, now is the time. Do not spend too much time debating this. Increase your fees for new clients and/or new matters immediately.

Still reluctant? This is a screenshot from Tiffany's website a few years ago. I am not sure if it is still available, but at one time, Tiffany's was selling this paper clip bookmark for $1,500. **FIFTEEN HUNDRED DOLLARS!**

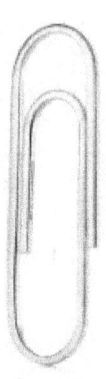

EVERYDAY OBJECTS
18k Gold Paper Clip
Bookmark

$1,500

You know people bought these. I promise there are clients willing to pay you what you are worth.

- Are you known as the "low-cost" option for your services?

Being the "low-cost" option for your services means you must become the volume leader. Volume quickly leads to burnout. I should know, I have been there.

It is not sustainable and it's not fun. You might be able to pull it off for a little while, but eventually, you will hit a wall. And when you do, take it from me, it is not pretty.

So, if you are known as the "low-cost" option, ask yourself this: is it worth it? Is sacrificing your sanity and your wellbeing worth a few extra bucks? Hint: the answer is no. Find another way to compete.

For years, I felt like my fees were decent. They were not the lowest nor the highest. I would say they were below the median for my local market.

I justified it in my head that I was providing honest and competent work to people who really needed it. Which was true. But, it came at a price: my mental and emotional wellbeing suffered.

At lower prices, I attracted clients who were not ideal for me. Clients who nitpicked every penny on my already low invoice. I had clients who would try to negotiate my prices with me like we were at a flea market. Uhm, what?!

Lower prices meant I needed to make up ground with volume. Volume meant cranking out work as fast as possible.

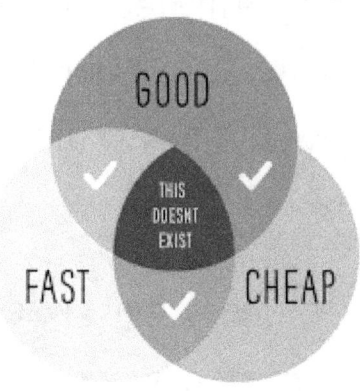

I was constantly under stress to make clients happy with fast turnaround times while listening to them complain about how "high" my fees were. Not an ideal situation for anyone. Clients were just as unhappy with me as I was with them.

It took a complete money mind shift to revamp my billing practices to value billing (not billing hourly!). I know that may seem radical for attorneys to adopt, but I do have a few clients who have their practice set up with value billing.

I am not suggesting you change away from your current billing structure. But, I am suggesting you review your fees and consider an increase for new matters and/or clients effective immediately.

- What would a 3% increase in your pricing mean for your profitability?

Take a moment to run the numbers. From your P&L for the last 12 months:

- Multiply your gross fee revenue by 3%. Add the resulting number to your net profit. How does a 3% increase in fees change your net profit for the year?
- Do the same calculations but change the 3% to 5%. What about a 5% increase?

> *3-5% increases will most likely be easily accepted by your current clients. If you decide to increase more than 5%, you may lose a handful of clients which may not be a bad thing as it frees up your capacity to work on remaining and new clients.*

Plan how you will implement your fee increase. Will you increase fees only on new matters starting today? Maybe only for new clients? Or for all clients and all matters starting at the end of the month?

Decide, notify clients, and move on. Do not agonize over this.

Margin

- When did you last analyze your profit margin?

Prior to Profit First, I advised all my professional service clients to have a target profit margin of 33%. From each dollar of revenue, 33% should be spent on wages for employees who directly support clients (e.g., revenue-generating employees), general overhead should be covered with the next 33%, and the final 33% going to your bottom line.

In other words:

Revenue 100% - Attorney & Paralegal wages (33%) - General Office Overhead (33%) = Net Profit (33%)

Now, with the Target Allocation Percentages (TAPs) provided for in the Profit First book, I work with clients to achieve the targets provided for in the book. I like that TAPs are adjusted based on Real Revenue as your firm grows.

I work together with my clients to make additional adjustments from the Profit First TAPs when appropriate. For example, almost none of my clients need to save 15% of Real Revenue for taxes. Do not confuse 15% of Real Revenue with a 15% effective tax rate. These are two completely different formulas.

The tax TAP is high on purpose, to guarantee that you have the money set aside to write checks to Uncle Sam when your tax bills are due. And, by saving a percentage of your Real Revenue for taxes, you are automatically covered if you experience a significant increase or decrease in revenue because your allocations match your current revenue levels.

When I can work with a client's tax advisor to get their effective tax rate, I am able to convert that to an appropriate tax TAP. From there, assuming the new tax TAP is below 15%, money has been freed up to be allocated elsewhere.

For example, if your tax TAP is more appropriate at 10%, that is 5% of your Real Revenue that can be allocated somewhere else (original 15% tax TAP - new 10% tax TAP = 5%).

For my firm, I allocated a portion of this tax savings money to a travel fund. I travel several times a year for in-person retreats with my mastermind group. Since everyone in the group is located throughout the US, we rotate to a new location with each retreat.

The remainder of this money, I allocated to employee perks such as tickets to sporting events, gift cards to fine dining establishments, or buying lunch for the office just because. It is important to me that my staff knows how appreciative I am of them.

If you are curious, I added two additional bank accounts for these: one for the travel fund and one for employee perks. I do not want the money to get "lost" in another bank account. I always know how much money I have available to spend on these dedicated expenses.

- Are you utilizing payment terms to their fullest?

For example, if a vendor offers you a 2% discount if you pay your bill within 10 days, do you leverage that?

If you are like most people, you probably think that a 2% discount may not be worth the hassle of trying to pay your bill within 10 days. After all, what's a couple of percent off when you're already paying full price?

However, there are a few things to consider before you write off the discount as not worth your time. First, every little bit helps. A 2% discount may not seem like much, but it can add up over time.

Second, if you are able to take advantage of the discount, it shows that you're a responsible customer who is willing to pay on time. This can give you a reputation as a good customer, which can lead to other benefits down the road from this vendor.

Alternatively, do you pay all your credit card balances in full every month to avoid finance charges? Do you pay bills on time to avoid late fees?

Many people carry a balance on their credit cards from month to month, incurring finance charges that can add up quickly. However, there are some simple steps you can take to avoid these charges.

First, make sure you pay your bill in full and on time every month. Late payments can result in additional fees, and if you only make the minimum payment, you'll be charged interest on the outstanding balance.

Second, keep an eye on your credit limit. If you exceed your credit limit, you will likely be charged a fee.

Finally, take advantage of any grace periods your card company offers. Most companies allow you to avoid finance charges if you pay your bill within a certain number of days after the due date.

By following these simple tips, you can reduce or eliminate finance charges. This in turn keeps money in your account.

I have worked with clients who routinely paid thousands of dollars a year in bank overdraft fees and over the limit credit fees. These were businesses that could not afford to lose that money. By implementing Profit First, we were able to manage cash, reduce debt and avoid paying those fees. It was the steppingstone to their survival.

- Do you use multiple providers for the same materials or services? Could you improve your margins (and your efficiency) by using fewer providers?

If you are like most businesses, you probably use a variety of different providers to purchase your supplies and services. But what if you could improve your margins by using fewer providers?

It might sound counter-intuitive, but it is quite simple.

When you use fewer providers, you have more negotiating power. You can get better deals and terms, which can save you money in the long run.

In addition, using fewer providers can help you streamline your operations and make them more efficient. So, before you sign up for that next service, pause to think about whether you really need it. It could be the difference between a successful business and one that just breaks even.

The two areas that stand out most times for law firms would be office supplies and continuing education. If you purchase all office supplies from one vendor, do they give you a volume discount? Same thing with continuing education.

Efficiency

- Is there anything in your business you are doing "because we've always done it that way?"

There may be processes that legitimately are the most efficient by doing them the way they have always been done. But, as technology changes, as the world changes, opportunities are everywhere to increase efficiency with updates to our processes.

Take a hard look at how things are done. Take the time to prepare Standard Operating Procedure documents (SOPs) for your processes. From lead generation and client onboarding to employee hiring and employee termination.

Seeing processes on paper can help you identify opportunities for improvement or weaknesses in your operations. Have someone independent from the SOP try to perform the steps for each SOP. Where did they get stuck? What did not make sense to them? Revised the SOP based on this feedback.

Personally, this is my least favorite thing to do. It is time intensive. But, the benefit is well worth the sacrifice. Make a list of processes and work on one SOP at a time until they are all done.

- Are you using the technology that is available to streamline processes in your business?

A few of my clients are early adopters when it comes to technology. I sometimes struggle to keep up with the latest software and equipment they use. I am not suggesting you become an early adopter, but instead consider how many spreadsheets, calendars, or notepads you are using to track stuff.

As anyone who is ever tried to get organized can attest, it is easy to let things slip through the cracks. Whether it is a Post-it note that gets lost in the shuffle, an appointment that gets double-booked or a file that gets inadvertently overwritten, it is all too easy to make a small mistake that can have big consequences. The good news is that there are ways to prevent these mishaps from happening in the first place.

Case management software will prioritize your workload based on dues dates. It will also alert you when a client's retainer balance is getting low or when payment has not been received on an invoice.

Client relationship management software will track leads and generate your engagement letter when they hire you at the push of a button.

Take time to demo software solutions that will replace manual and handwritten lists. I do not recommend any specific software because for me personally, most have the same features, but the user interface needs to appeal to me before I know I will use it. I feel that to be true for everyone.

Also, get your staff to review solutions with you too. The gesture to seek their opinion will empower them to help you grow your firm and make it easier to implement the solution when the time comes.

- Do you have team members working outside their zones of genius, when it could be more practical and cost-effective to outsource certain tasks to outside providers (VAs, marketing agencies, etc.)?

Do you have a paralegal who also posts to your social media accounts, updates your website, and handles your bookkeeping? It is possible that he or she excels at more tasks than a typical paralegal performs, but don't kid yourself.

If you are not already using part-time experts to help run your business, you're missing out on a huge opportunity. Not only are they faster and more efficient at their craft, but they also can keep you at the forefront of their zone of expertise.

> *"A man who represents himself has a fool for a client." - Abraham Lincoln*

The same principle applies here. You do not know what you don't know. Invest the money to work with an expert in the areas you need to manage your business.

By bringing in part-time experts, you will be able to tap into a wealth of knowledge and experience that you wouldn't otherwise have access to. And, because they are only working part-time, you'll save money on overhead costs as well.

So, what are you waiting for? Bring in some part-time experts and watch your business take off!

Leveraging Potential Client Interest

- Before they become a client – or even a prospect – potential clients visit your website and LinkedIn profiles. Are you tracking this activity? What are you doing to encourage these potential clients to become prospects and/or paying clients?

If you are like most business owners, you probably put a lot of time and effort into your website. You want it to be eye-catching and informative, and you want it to accurately reflect your brand. But once potential clients land on your website, what happens next? How are you tracking their movements and interactions? And more importantly, how are you converting those visitors into paying customers?

There are several ways to track potential clients who visit your website. One of the most popular methods is Google Analytics. This free tool provides detailed insights into website traffic, including where visitors come from, and which pages they interact with most. By understanding these patterns, you can make changes to your website that encourage visitors to take the next step in the process to convert them from a prospect to a qualified lead to a client.

- If you are tracking website traffic, when did you last conduct an A/B test to determine what yields the most interaction from your potential clients?

If you are not familiar with A/B testing, it's basically a way to compare two versions of something to see which one performs better.

For example, you could test two different headlines to see which one gets more clicks. A/B testing is a useful tool for any business because it can help you optimize your website or marketing materials for maximum effectiveness.

Conducting an A/B test is relatively simple; all you need is a goal (such as increased traffic or conversions) and two versions of whatever you're testing (such as two different headlines).

Once you have set up your test, you'll need to track the results to see which version performs better. A/B testing is an important part of any digital marketing strategy.

- Do you have a follow-up process to engage potential clients who start the prospect or onboarding process with you, but do not complete it?

As a business owner, you know the importance of follow-up. You would not dream of letting a hot lead slip through your fingers without staying in touch and trying to close the deal.

So why would you treat a potential client any differently? If someone starts the prospect or onboarding process with you but does not complete it, don't give up!

There are a few reasons why this might happen, and with a little follow-up, you can turn that interested prospect into a paying customer.

Here are a few tips for following up with potential clients who start but do not finish the prospect or onboarding process:

1. Check in to see if there was a problem with the process

If someone starts the prospect or onboarding process but does not finish, the first step is to check in and see if there was a problem with the process.

Did they get stuck on a certain task or question you asked? Did they not understand something?

There could be several reasons why they did not finish, and it is important to find out so you can address the issue and help them complete the process.

2. Find out if they are still interested

Even if there was not a problem with the process, it's possible that their interest has changed or that they've found another solution to their problem.

The best way to find out is to reach out and ask them directly.

3. See if there is anything you can do to help

If they are still interested, see if there is anything you can do to help them complete the process.

Sometimes all it takes is a little push in the right direction.

4. Follow up regularly

Finally, make sure you follow up with them on a regular basis. The exact frequency will depend on your business and relationship with the prospect, but a good rule of thumb is to follow up at least once a week until they either become a customer or it is clear that they're not interested.

Prospects

- How quickly do you respond to inquiries from prospective clients? How can you improve this response time? Hint: A quick response time results in higher closing rates.

When you are trying to win over a new client, timing is everything. The faster you can get in touch with a prospect, the better your chances are of closing the deal. In fact, research has shown that companies who respond to inquiries within an hour are seven times more likely to qualify the lead than those who wait more than an hour to respond.

If you want to close more deals, you need to make sure you are responding to prospective clients as quickly as possible.

There are a few different ways you can do this:

1. Use an autoresponder

One of the easiest ways to make sure you are responding quickly to inquiries is to set up an autoresponder. This way, anyone who emails you will receive a response right away, even if you are unavailable.

2. Check your email regularly

Another way to make sure you are responding quickly to inquiries is to check your email regularly. This way, you can reply to any new messages as soon as possible.

3. Use a CRM system

If you are handling a lot of inquiries, it may be helpful to use a CRM system. This way, you can keep track of all your conversations and make sure you are following up in a timely manner.

4. Hire an assistant

If you are really struggling to keep on top of your inquiries, you may want to consider hiring an assistant. This person can help you with tasks like responding to emails and incoming calls.

- Do you have a comprehensive follow-up process in place once you have made initial contact with a prospect?

If not, now is the time to put one together. By following up in a timely and professional manner, you will stand out from the competition and increase your chances of winning new business.

Although it may seem obvious, one of the best ways to stand out from the competition is to follow up in a timely and professional manner.

In today's business world, it is all too easy to let things slide - a client emails you with a question but you do not respond for a week, or you promised to send some additional information, but you never get around to it.

By following up promptly and keeping your commitments, you will make a lasting impression on potential clients and increase your chances of winning new business.

- What do you do with prospects who don't buy from you right away? Do you keep them engaged in any way?

There is always one lead who just won't commit. You have done everything right -

you've kept them engaged, you've sent them personalized messages, you've even thrown in a few extra benefits just for them. But still, they just will not hire you. So, what do you do with these leads?

Do not despair. Just because they are not buying from you right away doesn't mean they never will. They may just need a little more time to make their decision. In the meantime, there are a few things you can do to keep them engaged:

- Send them timely follow-ups. If they are interested in your services, they'll appreciate getting regular updates from you. Keep them engaged with timely follow-ups, relevant information, and personalized messages.

- Don't give up. Even if they do not hire you right away, there is a good chance they'll remember you when they're finally ready to make their decision.

New Clients

- Do you know your new client acquisition cost? When did you last seek to improve that cost?

Chances are you are always looking for ways to acquire new clients. But do you know what your new client acquisition cost is?

This is the amount of money you spend on marketing and advertising divided by the number of new clients you bring in. Once you know your new client acquisition cost, you can start to look for ways to improve it.

There are a few ways to do this, including making sure your marketing materials are targeted and effective, improving your sales process, and making sure your pricing is competitive.

By keeping an eye on your new client acquisition costs and constantly seeking ways to improve it, you can ensure that your business is always growing.

- What is your new client onboarding process? How might you improve this process so it is more efficient for your team and more pleasant for your client?

At my firm, we take new client onboarding seriously. We know that first impressions matter, and we want to make sure that our clients have the best possible experience working with us.

To that end, we have developed a comprehensive onboarding process that helps to ensure that both our team and our clients are well-prepared for the work ahead.

Of course, we are always looking for ways to improve the process, and we're open to suggestions from both our team and our clients.

After all, the goal is to make things as efficient and pleasant as possible for everyone involved.

- After a client engages you once, what do you do to either make them a repeat client, if possible depending on your area of practice, of course or encourage them to refer other clients to you?

There are a few things you can do to make sure your clients come back for more or recommend you to others.

First, always be on time and consistent with your appointments. Scheduling is one of the most difficult things to keep track of, especially when you have a lot of clients, but it is important to be as reliable as possible.

If you say you are going to meet with a client at 2 pm, make sure you are there at 2 pm. And if for some reason you cannot make it, let them know as soon as possible so they can plan accordingly.

Second, always be prepared for your meetings.

This means having all the relevant information and documents on hand so you can address any questions or concerns they might have. If you are constantly having to run back to the office or look things up online, it is going to reflect poorly on you.

Third, keep them updated on their case - let them know what is going on and what to expect next. Failing to communicate with your clients is one of the quickest ways to lose business. People want to work with attorneys who keep them in the loop and make them feel like they're a priority.

Finally, say thank you - a little appreciation goes a long way! A kind word or gesture can really make someone's day. It does not have to be anything major - just a simple "thank you" by email, a phone call or a handwritten card dropped in the mail can brighten someone's day and let them know you appreciate them as a client.

By following these simple steps, you can create lasting relationships with your clients and ensure they will keep coming back for more. Maintaining a healthy client base is essential to the success of any law firm, so do not take your clients for granted. Show them that you value their business and their trust in you by giving them the best possible service.

Matters

- Do you know your average matter revenue amount? When did you last analyze this?

It is no secret that law firms are always looking for ways to increase their revenues. But did you know that one of the easiest ways to do this is to simply focus on your average matter revenue amount?

This is the average amount of revenue that you generate per matter, and it can have a big impact on your bottom line. Of course, the first step is to calculate this number. Luckily, it is not too difficult to do.

Simply divide your total revenue for the year by the number of matters that you handled during that same period. Once you have your average matter revenue amount, it is time to start analyzing it.

Look at your biggest cases and see if there are any commonalities. Are they all in the same practice area? Do they have the same originating attorney?

If you see any commonalities, you can use that information to adjust your marketing and business development efforts. For example, if you find that most of your big cases come from referrals from other attorneys, you might want to focus on building relationships with other attorneys in your practice area.

If you see that most of your big cases originate from one attorney in your firm, you might want to talk to that attorney about how they are generating business and see if there are any lessons you can learn.

- Do you suggest upsells or cross-sells for additional services to encourage higher average transaction amounts? How might you leverage this?

As much as they may seem like one in the same, there is a subtle difference between upselling and cross selling that can make all your marketing efforts more successful.

Upselling occurs when you offer a client additional service to improve their current situation. It is upsizing your order at McDonald's. In the legal world, upselling could include offering trust formation services for a client looking to create a will, for example.

Cross-selling is different. When you are cross-selling, you're offering a whole new set of legal services. A client comes to you for a divorce, and you offer to update his/her estate plan as well. The key to identifying cross-selling opportunities is to engage clients to learn about their life, their business, and their needs.

- Do you know your average cost per transaction? How might you reduce this cost without compromising the client experience? (Analyze merchant service fees, improve team efficiencies, etc.)

Other than your wage costs, do you have additional costs per transaction? For example, do you accept credit card payments from clients? Did you know that ACH payments from clients are generally

cheaper to process than a credit card
transaction for the same amount?

Marketing ROI

- Do you know your ROI on each marketing initiative you have in your business? Which marketing activity has the highest ROI?

Do you know the return on investment for each marketing initiative in your business? Being aware of your ROI for each marketing campaign allows you to make smart decisions about where to allocate your resources. Do you know what ROI you are getting for each marketing activity in your business? If not, now is the time to find out.

- How do you track your marketing ROI? Do you have a system in place? Does each team member know how to use and update the system?

There are a few key ways to track your marketing ROI.

First, look at your website traffic. See how many visitors are coming to your site, and where they are coming from. This will give you an idea of which marketing channels are bringing in the most traffic.

Next, look at your revenue numbers. See how many clients and matters you are billing, and how much revenue you are generating. This will help you see which marketing campaigns are resulting in the most revenue.

Finally, do not forget to track your client satisfaction levels. See how satisfied your clients are with your services. This will help you see which marketing campaigns are resulting in the happiest clients.

- What are your marketing habits? Do you only advertise when business is slow, or do you market consistently and keep your sales funnel full?

Do you have any specific marketing habits that you follow on a regular basis? Perhaps you always start your day by posting on your business socials, drafting a new blog post each week, or maybe you make it a point to attend networking events once or twice a month. Whatever your marketing habits may be, they can have a big impact on your firm's success.

Accounts Receivable

- What is your average time to collect client invoices? Do you have a process in place to quickly follow up on past due invoices?

The longer it takes for a client to pay, the lower of a priority it will become for them to pay you. Collectability is reduced a little bit every day.

- Do you make it easy for clients to pay you? For example, do you provide a payment link on your invoices so clients can pay with a credit card or ACH transaction?

You want them to have a good experience with your business, and that starts with paying you. How can you streamline the process so that it is easy and frictionless for your clients?

- Rather than letting clients pay in arrears, could you use retainers to help with your accounts receivable process?

There are a few options for handling payment when working with clients. One option is to allow them to pay in arrears. Another option is to use retainers. Retainers can help to ensure that you are paid on time and in full for your services. If you are considering using retainers, be sure to discuss this with your clients in advance so that they are aware of your policy and can plan accordingly.

Which Profit Point did you find to be the most profound to your business?

So, what is your next step? It may be overwhelming to read all of the Profit Points, but please pick any one of the Profit Points and start making small changes in your business today. You may be surprised at how much of an impact even a few small tweaks can have on your bottom line.

Thank you so much for reading Stop Struggling and Start Thriving: A Guide To Transform Your Law Firm! It means the world to me that you chose to spend some time with inside the book.

With that said, I would love to hear personally what you thought of the book!

You can look me up on LinkedIn (**linkedin.com/in/kelleybrubakercpa/**) or email me (**kelley@ProfitScaleThrive.com**) and let me know your thoughts on the book.

And if you want to take things to the next level, my team and I are here to help. We would love to work with you to assist with implementing Profit First in your firm or work on other areas for improvement. Reach out to us today at **ProfitScaleThrive.com/contact**.

About The Author

While I am a Certified Public Accountant (CPA) and not an attorney, our firms are managed identically. Hourly billings. Hard deadlines. High client expectations with sometimes impossible circumstances.

For more than a decade now, a significant portion of my client base has been law firms. I know firsthand the issues with managing the work with limited staffing. Having amazing billing months but waiting for months to collect from clients. Investing in expert witnesses with high retainers and carrying that cost until the case is settled.

In my own firm, in the beginning, I tried to solve every problem I possibly could for every client that walked in my door – even problems that were not part of my zone of genius. And it crushed me.

I worked 10 to 12 hours a day 6 to 7 days a week and at the end of the year, my net profit was barely over $100,000. I hired staff to help. I still worked the same ridiculous hours and my net profit dropped because I increased my overhead faster than I was increasing my revenue. As a result, I made just enough to pay for my kids to be in daycare while I was at work.

*What the f*ck was I doing to myself?*

Fast forward a couple of years and a neighbor of mine who was also a small business owner recommended the book "Profit First" by Mike Michalowicz. At the time I did not have time to read the book, but I bought it and put it on my bookshelf to be read *someday*.

At this point in my life, I was wrapped up in raising my babies. So, sadly it took me another few years before I made time to read the book. The general concept was something I had discussed with my small business owners for years! It was easy for me to understand the book. It was so simple; it was brilliant!

I began listening to Mike's podcast while I did chores around the house. It amazed me that such a simple concept could be so profound for a small business.

After a few months of implementing Profit First in my firm, I investigated becoming a Profit First Professional. I needed to start sharing this with my clients. My only regret is that I did not become a Profit First Professional sooner!

Being a Profit First Professional has given me the knowledge and tools to immensely change how I manage my firm which, in turn, improved my life outside of my firm. And now, I can show you how to implement Profit First in your firm too.

Above all, I believe that family comes first and that my business should be a tool for improving the lives of those I love most. That includes running a business that provides time flexibility, financial freedom, and joy.

Free Resources

Several resources were referenced in the book as being available for download. To download these resources, please visit the following page:

https://mailchi.mp/profitscalethrive.com/ stop-struggling-resources

Enjoying Disneyland with my daughters - Spring Break 2023

www.ingramcontent.com/pod-product-compliance
Lightning Source LLC
Chambersburg PA
CBHW062329290526
45794CB00005B/1958